THE SECRET OF BEING HAPPY

ALDIVANTEIXEIRA TORRES

Copyright © 2019 by AldivanTeixeira Torres.

ISBN   978-1-970160-58-1 Ebook
ISBN   978-1-970160-59-8 Paperback

All rights reserved. No part of this publication may be reproduced, distributed, or transmitted in any form or by any means, including photocopying, recording, or other electronic or mechanical methods without the prior written permission of the publisher. For permission requests, solicit the publisher via the address below through mail or email with the subject line "Attention: Publication Permission".

EC Publishing LLC
11100 SW 93rd Court Road, Suite 10-215
Ocala, Florida 34481-5188, USA

Ordering Information:
Quantity sales. Special discounts are available on quantity purchases by corporations, associations, and others. For details, contact the publisher at the address above.

www.ecpublishingllc.com
info@ecpublishingllc.com
+1 (352) 234-6201

Printed in the United States of America

CONTENTS

Dedication and thanks xi
Introduction xv

The Administrator 1
The case of Richard Koll and Selena Beck 4
A life marked by fantastic turns 6
The economist president 9
Foreign Trade Professional 11
A profession that gives priority to elites 14
The Third World War 16
Overcoming Preconceptions 17
Have attitude to change 19
An example of heroism 21
The flower 23
A marketing expert 24
An angel on earth 25
The pleasure allied to the profession 26
A master of world architecture 27
A complete artist 29
A renowned artist 32
An unforgettable actress 34
A singer who marked the season 36

Conservation and restoration 38
Dance 39
The precursor of Brazilian design 40
Photography 42
A respected physicist 43
A genius named Newton 45
In the computer age 46
A Remarkable Naturalist 47
Mathematical and land sciences 49
A renowned statistician 50
The modern medicine 51
The father of modern chemistry 52
A fantastic archaeologist 53
The value of cooperation 54
A great jurist 55
A joke to others 57
A black symbol 58
An ethno development activist 59
Socrates 60
A famous geographer 61
Historian 62
A little bit of the little dreamer of the cave 63
A leading museologist 66
The patron of Brazilian education 67
Psychopedagogy 69
International relations 70
Social worker 71
An ancient theologian 72
A recognized Baiano translator 74
Archivist 75
Librarian 76
Cinema and audiovisual 77
The edu-communicator 79
Bachelor of Media Studies 80

Information management 81
A renowned journalist 82
Multimedia 84
Cultural producer 85
Editorial Producer 86
Advertising 87

Short Biography: Aldivan Teixeira Torres, born in Arcoverde-PE-Brazil, develops the series of novels "the seer", poetry, books of the genre self-help, religious, the field of wisdom, among others. To date it has published titles in Portuguese, Spanish, English, French and Italian. From an early age, he has always been a lover of the art of writing and has consolidated a professional career since the second semester of 2013. He hopes to contribute to the Pernambuco and Brazilian culture, arousing the pleasure of reading in those who do not have the habit. Your mission is to win the heart of each of your readers. Besides literature, his main tastes are music, travel, friends, family and the very pleasure of living. "For literature, equality, fraternity, justice, dignity and honor of the human being always" is his motto.

DEDICATION AND THANKS

I dedicate this book to all the workers who jointly collaborate for the development of the country. Big or small, they play an important role.

Thank you for another achievement to God in the first place, my family, my co-workers, my friends, acquaintances, admirers of my work and those who encourage national literature. Let's make this country a place of full culture.

"Work is love made visible. And if you cannot work with love, but only with disgust, it is better to leave work, sit at the door of the temple and take alms to those who work with joy."

(Khalil Gibran)

INTRODUCTION

The secret of being happy brings some of the most important professions of the current scenario in relation to the labor market. More than a guide for students and scholars in general, it is an essential text in the search for your professional identity. I wish you all a good reading.

The author

THE ADMINISTRATOR

Henry Rafaz has always been a young man integrated into the social, technological and financial world. A middle class native, he saw the opportunity to specialize in a college. He chose Administration with the certainty of the world. Since he lived in São Paulo, the opportunities in the labor market would not be lacking.

During the graduation period, he sought more information about his area. According to the research, the administrator was responsible for managing the material resources, financial or human resources of the company. The field of activity of this professional is in public or private organizations acting in virtually all departments. The essential prerequisite is knowing how to drive the business goals, which involves planning, executing, correcting, controlling and analyzing results. With the knowledge gained in college and his own experience, he would know exactly how to act in situations of risk or bonanza. Thank God, he had made the right choice.

This four-year period in which he improved his professional side was also rich on the personal side: He had a good relationship, he expanded contacts, he had good and bad aggregating experiences, learned a little more of life and religion, strolled and reflected. What remains of all this has been the certainty that life is a great challenge and that the way of dealing with it completely changes its meaning. Hence the sense of having the administration as a profession. At the end of this time, he finished his university studies, got married and started planning the next steps of his life.

Life for two is one of the biggest challenges a couple can have. Henry and Marcela were experiencing this phase after two years of dating and engagement. The two met in the college cafeteria and it was love at first sight. Who took the initiative was her to approach, to introduce themselves and to ask for information about the city. Marcela was a native of Porto Seguro-Bahia and moved to São Paulo because of family problems. Her pale skin, her pale face, her sculpted body, and her large eyes were something that immediately caught the attention of the young administrator. Showing himself kind and solicitous, he gave warm tips and advice on the city and the people in general. How sympathetic to her, she provided him at the end of the conversation with his personal phone number and his social networks. From this day on, the meetings began, exchanged the first kisses and hugs, officialized the courtship and later, the engagement. Now they were married having to reconcile their personal interests which was not easy. Luckily, they were already stabilized. They were the modern type of couple in which both worked and cared for the household chores. By common agreement, they had plans to grow further.

Their next step was to plan to have children. As it was their will, they had three babies. Unable to take care of them directly for professional reasons, they hired a trustworthy nanny named Rebecca who was Marcela's cousin. At the same time, they continued to specialize in their respective professions: Administration and Linguistics. Everything in their lives was well except for contact with their children. But it was a necessary choice for their own good. This is a common reality in families set in the big city.

The children grew up, the couples were getting high positions in their areas which was a source of pride for the whole family. They had stumbled but they managed to get up again.

Some time later, they retired and formed their children living in full happiness. It is clear that whoever prepares and is a good professional will always have his place in the job market even though we are experiencing a catastrophic crisis. Experts are unanimous in saying that what is missing is qualification for the Brazilian worker. Fortunately it is not the case of this couple presented who knew how to overcome difficulties, find solutions, plan every stage of their life. Despite having unforeseen events, the important thing is to have a starting point and not despair. If you are the idealizing type, the management course is perfect for your dreams.

THE CASE OF RICHARD KOLL AND SELENA BECK

Richard and Selena were born and raised in the same region of downtown Toronto-Canada. Since they were small, they have always maintained contact because the families have a close relationship of friendship. The boy used to be the stereotype of the spoiled, irresponsible, liberal young man. His tender way of being caught the girl's attention. Besides that, he was handsome, handsome and handsome. It certainly was a challenge for any girl who cared about her honor. Is it possible to conquer such an untamed heart? This was the object of that passionate girl.

Due to their closeness, many opportunities appeared for her to declare her love, but her desire always ran up against her timidity and the possible reaction of her parents. She was almost certain that her relationship would not be accepted because of the boy's unpretentious way of being and the fact that he belonged to an aristocratic, principled family. In this way, the days went by and the situation between the days remained the same: A beautiful friendship.

At one point, there was a radical change in Richard's life: He took his wits and went to the family business to go and live inside the province on his parents' ranch. With that decision, the contact with *the family of the girl was scarce. Full of nostalgia, the young woman took advantage and invented any excuse to visit her beloved secret.*

In the day and time combined, the meeting happened and they talked a lot. The young man spoke about his future plans and even commented on the dream of arranging a marriage. It was there that she took advantage and revealed her desire to know him better. To his surprise, he returned, giving her a kiss and a hug. Thus began the official courtship between the two for the general happiness of all.

Together, they built a clean, discreet, promising and loving relationship. Following his dream, Rich joined the faculty of agribusiness and agriculture. This had everything to do with his current function at the farm that was to manage the administrative, financial, economic and social aspects related to agricultural and livestock production activities. In four years, he completed his training and was already able to officially assume these responsibilities. Of breaking, he engaged and soon afterwards got married. His moody neighbor was really his soul mate. About this he was sure. Their plans involved having children, acquiring business and home ownership, traveling extensively, and growing old together. Surely they deserved to be happy forever.

A LIFE MARKED BY FANTASTIC TURNS

Katty Green is a North American resident in the state of Texas. With humble origins and black skin, from early she suffered prejudice and discrimination in a very intense way. Maybe if you're rich and white you do not know how to scale what she's been through, but it's really something to worry about in a society that's evolved and globalized like ours.

Born in the seventies, a period still apartheid with massive dominance of white males and high social class. Being black, woman, and poor at this time was really a tremendous lack of luck. There was a high degree of separation between socially accepted groups and minorities.

She was born in a small neighborhood on the outskirts of the capital, the oldest of seven children. Her father was killed by drug traffickers when she was seven years old, which forced her and her mother to work as a diarist in high-concept homes in the center. It starts there a little of the nightmare that was your life.

At the age of fifteen she spent working on household chores, she was beaten, defamed and even raped. However, it was a decent job just like any other. The problem is many people who do not have principles and feel they own the world. Certainly their fate is not good.

After this period, she made a decision that completely changed her life. She prepared everything and on a beautiful night of the full moon left the house. Before you criticize her, think that she was tired of the problems and poverty she faced. Her brothers were grown up and could live alone. Running away was the only solution to try to change your routine and try to find a new path.

What she did not know was that the world was far worse than she thought. The first few days she had passed out on the street suffering hunger, cold and contempt. One day she was rescued by a stranger who promised her a job in the noble area of the city. Lively and with new perspectives, she followed the stranger. She was housed in a really luxurious farmhouse where she served as a waitress, singer and dancer. The worst moment was to find out that she would also act as a sexual escort.

Why? What had she done wrong for life to be so unlucky? She had always been a good person, applied to work, sincere, understanding, and trusting in God. The color of her social class did not define her at all. It was still little Katty who had learned from her parents the right values to follow. She did not know for sure, but she could not be discouraged at the moment because she would always believe in God's providence especially because she was well in need.

As the beautiful story goes, faith always wins and everything has its time. The happiness of this young woman happened when she met in her work a nice young businessman. When they talked for a while, he was delighted by her and immediately invited her to live with him. For this dream to come true, he bought her rights and freed her from captivity. He took her home and started life together. The beautiful black woman began to study and as she was very intelligent she advanced all levels of American education with very high concepts. She was selected for the best university in her state where she went to study accounting. The function of the accountant is to take care of the accounting part of the company through records and control of revenues, expenses and profits. The scope of the work involves purchases, investments and actions giving a broad view of the equity. This profession was perfect for her who already had experience in home economics.

Katty improved her life both financially and personally. On a return to the past, she visited her family and watched them best. There was no need to apologize for what she did, just a glance to understand that she had never forgotten and loved them very much. The trajectory was now different. The lesson is that nothing is definitive. Nothing is so bad that it cannot change.

THE ECONOMIST PRESIDENT

Diana Morales is a world-renowned figure representing the democratic institution in a developing continent. Her story is permeated with pain, struggles, worthy desires, blunt personal experiences that have shaped her dignified and human character.

From an early age, she had an interest in participating in the political movement of her country by moving against authoritarian and undemocratic regimes. This rebellion cost her persecution, torture and a few years in prison. With the country in a somewhat more stable situation, her family was released and reintegrated. Then she went on with her life. She married, had children and graduated in economics which is an area that studies the production and distribution of goods and services in society in general among people, companies or nations. It was a preparation for her future as a citizen in its broadest sense.

Soon after, she returned to act in politics occupying important positions becoming minister of the republic. It was not long before she was invited to be president. She accepted the challenge, she was elected and with her academic experience made good progress for her country. Among the main ones, we can mention: Real increase in the minimum wage; Increased investment in public education; Scholarships for the needy youth; modernization of ports and airports; Greater middle-class access to consumer goods and leisure events; Promotion of industry and trade with record production of automobiles; Improvements in international relations with expansion in the flow of foreign trade; improvement in the income of the worker in general; Greater access of ordinary citizens to banking networks; A good value in international reserves; Financing of the state bank with zero defaults and inflation within the programmed targets.

In a globalized world, it is normal that there are crises and challenges. However, one person cannot be held responsible for the current situation in a country. One should rather combat corruption that is a dangerous evil for all. We must, as the saying goes, take away the rotten fruits so as to leave the good ones. In the day that happens we can be sure that a nation will be on the right track.

Diana for being competent and effective aroused much envy of her adversaries who, using constitutional prerogatives, removed her from the position of president. If this is going to solve the problem we do not know but it is up to us to recognize the great role that this woman represents in the world scenario. We have no doubt of its competence being affected by political-financial circumstances. Good luck to her.

The economics course is suitable for people with an innovative profile and who want to transform a reality that can act in the private or public area.

FOREIGN TRADE PROFESSIONAL

Peter Kall was born into a middle-class family in London-England. He was a healthy, sturdy, handsome, and promising boy. As soon as he came into the world, he was welcomed by his family with joy and satisfaction as he was the eldest son of Estefanny and Andrew Hoffman.

They lived in a middle-class neighborhood of the capital where they had access to almost everything: schools, supermarkets, cinema, theater, bar, parks, stadiums, pharmacies. Etecetera. From a young age, the young boy enjoyed the comfort of a home, of familiar warmth, of good financial and psychological conditions.

Until one day at school more specifically in the men's toilet he was drawn to witnessing a boy urinating. This experience he kept for himself because he was afraid of the reaction of the people who lived with him. It was also too early to think about his sexual side because he was only twelve years old.

Time passed a little and he grew. He became a handsome young man, acculturated, optimist, warrior, a really nice person. Even wanting to hide from his impulses, the image of the boy urinating still filled his mind making him think of something more concrete. It was trying to find his sexual identity that he left with a boy and a girl. With the girl, he did not pass the preliminaries finding it all very annoying. Already with the boy he liked it a lot and as he was experienced it made him feel in the seventh heaven. It was shameful to admit but despite everything he could face that he was homosexual. Unlike most people think, it was not a question of choice, but rather an orientation that he had brought from his conception of something larger in terms of genetics suits.

The first goal had been achieved. Now, he had two options: Deny this important part of his life because sex is health or take over. As he was a young battler, he chose the second option. From discovery he went on to planning how and when to reveal his identity to his parents. After much thinking, he decided to talk to them right on his birthday. This was done. At a gathering attended by those closest to him, he celebrated the most important date of his life. When it all calmed down, he summoned his parents and the three of them moved into a reserved room. Speaking gently, he explained his situation and his wishes, concluding that he loved them very much. At this moment, something seems to have broken down, their parents changed color and they lowered their heads in disgust. How could their boy of such a good family could lend himself to such a thing? Speaking rudely, they were unanimous in not accepting and nonconformists resolved to expel the child from home. They simply did not want any more contact with that freak. This word they named their beloved son.

Full of pain and despair, Peter was forced to pack his bags and when they were ready he left without a destination. It was night and he had no idea what to do or where to go. He thought for a minute, used his cell phone, and called his aunt for an address for a few days. He did not go into detail but mentioned that he had family problems. Lucky for him, his aunt accepted him, and then he went to his house a few blocks away. The first problem was partially solved. Life was going to follow with him guarding wounded marks of his past life. Maybe he was never the same.

Aunt Evellyn was a lovely person because she knew how to understand his reasons and welcome him. But he knew he had to act immediately so he would not be dependent on the others. Delivering resumes in the neighborhood, he had some job offers. He ended up finding a job as a waiter. With the salary, he could move from his aunt's house and gain his independence. That's exactly what he did. Concomitantly, he attended college entrance examination and as he was very intelligent and prepared he went on the busy foreign trade course. This professional understands the methods of buying and selling products and services, between companies and governments of diverse countries. When graduating in this area, this young man had the opportunity to stabilize himself in the labor market and realize his dreams.

One of his trips abroad was that he knew his great love. Ricardo, Portuguese from Lisbon, a tall brunette, slim, slim body, light brown eyes, soft skin. He was an international ambassador and fell in love at first sight. They met for a while, traveled extensively together and agreed to live in Paris, away from the evil looks of both families. They were aware that they could not have everything, but just having each other's company they would enjoy immense happiness.

Time has advanced, they have grown older, studied harder, and have adopted some children. Their happiness then was complete. They were a family with full rights like any other and would not allow anyone to humiliate or despise them. All the dark past was left behind. Now they would be lords of their own history until death do them part.

A PROFESSION THAT GIVES PRIORITY TO ELITES

We were in São Paulo in the eighties. The couple formed by Rodrigo Silva and Samanta Teixeira were struggling to survive in a big city. From the Northeast, the first one was metallurgical, and the second one was caring for the elderly in an asylum. What they earned was barely enough to survive, but compared to the catastrophic reality the north-east lived on it was much better.

At one point, both of them lost their jobs and because they did not have enough professional qualifications, a job placement would not be easy. They even tried a few times, but every time the answer was negative. Without alternatives, they decided to return to their land in search of new horizons.

Arriving there, they used labor indemnity money to open a small business, an assortment of groceries. If all went well, they could support themselves and their three young children. Because they were hard-working, things began to thrive. The children grew up with different goals. One was applied to the studies, another one more related to the businesses of the family and the third one was deficient.

Barbara was the name of the girl who was an example

of dedication to school. It was the pride of the family. Her sister retired and her brother followed in the family business. Calculator, sensible, beautiful and smart, soon caught everyone's eye. She chose as faculty to study the actuarial sciences that is a branch that uses the knowledge and calculations to elaborate plans of insurance or pension and realization of other financial operations that involve risk. As she chose correctly and was well applied, she was successful and soon got a good job placement in a bank.

As soon as she began to work, little by little, she was fulfilling her dreams and those of the family. This was a prize for all the joint effort they had in life. But as not everything can be obtained, she was unhappy in the personal life. Her dream, as any woman, was to marry but because of the circumstances and her temper she was never able to understand with anyone. She's still in the fight for her soul mate, but maybe she's probably never going to make it. The most important thing she has achieved: Personal satisfaction, stability and independence. Good luck to her.

THE THIRD WORLD WAR

We are in the year 2050. The world is covered by the fear, despair and darkness of a new world-wide clash. The reason for this is the dispute for natural resources, more specifically the only forest reserve in the world that still holds much of its original coverage, the Amazon jungle. On one side of the litigation is the Western conglomerate involving Brazil, USA, Mexico, Portugal, and Argentina and on the other the Eastern conglomerate with participation from China, Japan, Germany and Australia.

While the first group defends the Brazilian territorial hegemony the other attacks with arguments that the Amazon is universal. In the first attacks, three Brazilians were assassinated and the Brazilian territory was occupied by the foreigners which triggered an immediate reaction and the formation of the blocks. In this situation, the work of the bachelor in strategic and international management is present. This professional is responsible for formulating and executing strategic public policies for the defense of society. Thanks to his father, Brazil is a country rich in human resources and has pledged the best professionals to defend the country. Allied with American technology, he responded firmly to the enemies by driving them out of their territory. Due to the worldwide commotion towards the end of the war and by the few possibilities to react, the Eastern group surrendered. The world was safe again.

OVERCOMING PRECONCEPTIONS

Estevão Balzack was born in the municipality of Canindé do São Francisco, state of serjipe-Brazil. The strong, delicate, cunning and loving boy learned early on the separation of professional functions between man and woman. The man must provide for the household while the woman must take care of the children and the house. However, he was never satisfied with this regional taboo because he always liked some things that were not well recommended for the man. He felt himself bound by his own will.

The economy of his city was not so good that it killed his family in situation of critical necessity. He had learned carpentry from his father, and that was all he knew how to do. One day, in a sincere conversation, he asked permission to try a new life in the Southeast where it was said that the economy was more developed and consequently with more opportunity to work. No way out, his father named Meldezeck authorized and then planned this trip. He would stay in the house of a cousin who lived in Mauá.

With everything ready, the little Sergipe launched into this adventure in search of better living conditions. When he arrived in the state of São Paulo, he marveled and was enchanted by everything he saw and heard. The Southeast was an advanced region in economic and behavioral terms. In the typical family of São Paulo, generally all of working age worked and helped themselves in the housework. With more freedom, he could then dedicate himself not only to the work of a carpenter but to carry on with his studies. He chose the gastronomy faculty that is recommended for those who have creativity in the confection of food in the areas of confectionery, baking and in the different types of cuisine: Japanese, Northeastern, Sao Paulo, Chinese, European or elsewhere.

He successfully completed the course and was employed in a restaurant. With the good salary he earned he can then help his parents and himself. In a short time, he managed to open his own business and became one of the most recommended professionals in the state and country. This proves that there should be no bias and no division of activities between men and women. One should rather follow what one likes to be able to feel happy and fulfilled just like the example quoted.

HAVE ATTITUDE TO CHANGE

Karine was a tall, chubby black girl born and living in the Campinas-SP region. Created with love and affection by the parents, from an early age she learned the values of coexistence in a society and of personal fulfillment. She also learned very hard how the world through people is evil. She suffered in her skin the prejudice of being a woman, black and fat. The world is even a place of hypocritical people who thinks they own the world.

Instinctively, a revolt grew in her and she decided to make a difference. At all times, she fought for her rights and for others. This warrior spirit made her choose the career of public policy management. This course has activities related to the diagnosis, planning, execution and evaluation of actions and policies established by the government in all spheres. It is the problem-solving mechanism of strategic government areas such as health, education, social assistance, housing, leisure, transportation, security and the environment. This professional can act as manager in secretaries in any sphere as well as in companies and public administration bodies.

Her strength, courage and faith led her to complete her course and pass a well-contested contest. She started acting as a state manager in her area. Through innovative projects, it was possible to change the lives of minorities and it became recognized and respected around the world. She showed the strength and competence of the Brazilian black woman. In addition, she married, she had children and can teach them everything he has learned. Always make a difference.

AN EXAMPLE OF HEROISM

Maicon had been born to be personal security. Grown up in the Rio de Janeiro favela, he never compromised with the injustices he witnessed throughout his childhood. He saw many crimes without public power being able to react or when he reacted he was bribed by financial power. This sense of impotence of public security touched his heart in such a way that when he grew up he decided to act in the area as a personal protector.

But he was not any angel. He was highly prepared to perform his duties. Graduated from the federal university, he learned all the defense techniques needed to perform his duties. The course chosen outside private security management. Who has this training is a technologist specialized essentially in property and personal security. This professional identifies and analyzes safety risks by defining action and prevention guidelines. The field of activity is in the security, value transport and escort companies, in the protection of assets and facilities of industries, purchasing centers and companies in general.

Soon he got a job placement. He was acting as the personal guard of an important businessman. One delicate moment that passed was when a group of thieves surrounded the car they were in. There was a reaction and consequently an exchange of shots. Thieves gave up the action. However, Maicon was seriously injured. He had to go through surgery with a slow recovery. Thanks to his father he survived and his master was eternally grateful for his act of heroism. More than an employee, he was his friend. He remained in office, contracted marriage, had children, and grew old with health. He went through other dangerous situations inherent in his profession but for him it did not matter. What was worth was that he was happy to do good and defend justice. So he was happy until the rest of his days.

THE FLOWER

Ana Klara was a nice girl from the neighborhood, Boa Viagem in Recife. Raised in a middle-class family, she showed up early from her early days as well as working well with the visitors at her residence. Her kindness was so great that she earned the flower's nickname.

Due to her abilities she gave a college entrance exam to the hotel area. Who is formed in this is responsible for the direction and operation of hotels, resorts, inns, spas, flats and resorts coordinating accommodation, food, recreation and leisure services. You can also work in hospitals or in shopping centers. When making the right choice, she performed in the Professional Field acting in a luxury hotel. There, she was able to practice everything she had learned at graduation. She was happy to be useful to society. The flower's name was known all over Great Recife, and everyone spoke very highly of it.

A MARKETING EXPERT

Pedro Trevo since childhood showed up with a gift for interpersonal relationships. In order to help support his low-class family, he came out selling popsicles, pastries, and even juggling crossroads to get attention and win some change. At no point has he ever complained of overwork or of his condition.

When growing up, he chose as a profession the area of marketing including graduation. The attribution of this professional consists of seeking to increase sales of a particular business. Its role is to detect and seize the market opportunities attracting the consumer. It also elaborates strategies to gain the loyalty of a certain public as well as maintain a good image of a product. This had everything to do with his profile.

Upon completing the course, he was asked to work in a large international automobile company. He has made a career, he has become an executive and then can reward his family for trust, investment made and understanding by regular removal from home. He was a great man, master of his art, happy in his choices and accomplished by achieving his goals.

AN ANGEL ON EARTH

Eduardo Simon is a living example of courage, of struggle for minorities, of goodwill, intelligence and detachment. His background is in public safety. This area is recommended for those who have a sense of justice and want to fight against injustice and violence. The functions of this worker include deep understanding of the country's security problems and understanding their position in this regard for the benefit of society by implementing public policies.

He became the guardian of the lives of everyone in his community by proposing projects to improve security as a whole. His role is exemplary in the repression of organized crime and drug trafficking in a favela known in the capital of São Paulo. If everyone followed his example, we would have more national success against the evil group.

He is a brave instrument of God that carries the values of the full man. This is learned in the family context and spreads to the benefit of others. All, good and bad, have been children. Proper treatment on the ground can rid many of the world's criminality and wickedness. Allied with a good economic policy can provide a perfect environment of peace and harmony on earth. Let us perpetuate this example and believe that the world still has a solution.

THE PLEASURE ALLIED TO THE PROFESSION

Karen Switch is a nifty North American whose greatest pleasure is traveling. She also enjoys British Rock, theater, cinema, literature and sports. The experience gained in the various places in which it has been expanded its culture and enriched its vision of the world. At a certain point in her life, already married and having two children, she decided to take a definitive course in her life. She gave a university entrance exam for Tourism. She was approved and with what she learned in college she can ally her great passion to her profession. This bachelor does the planning, organization, promotion and dissemination of leisure points and their events. You can work in operating agencies, tourist sites, hotels, event companies or in leisure areas.

She had to leave her husband and children for her dreams but she did not care because they were already raised. In this life no one has possession of anything and life has to be used in all its moments. At least once a month, she visited them, killing the miss. She was an agent of an international tourist company, and this position enabled her to travel further, her great dream. So she lived until she retired. She returned home and can tell her stories to her children, grandchildren and great-grandchildren. When she died, she took with her only the good works.

A MASTER OF WORLD ARCHITECTURE

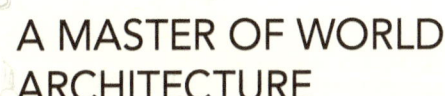

Oscar Ribeiro De Almeida Niemeyer Soares Filho was a great Brazilian architect considered an important figure in the development of modern architecture. His being of analytical perception and his creativity have made him a great genius of his area. The architect is responsible for designing and organizing internal and external spaces making the plant and determining the materials that can be used.

Niemeyer's best-known projects were made in Brasilia, a city planned and built to be the capital of the country. He also collaborated with other architects for the construction of the headquarters of the United Nations in New York, in the United States of America. The characteristics of his work exploring the constructive possibilities of reinforced concrete influenced the world of architecture. Inspired by the work of Le Corbusier, he became known as a sculptor of monuments.

Born in Rio de Janeiro, he studied at the National School of Fine Arts, graduating in the third year with Lúcio Costa, with whom he later collaborated in the construction project of the state's Ministry of Education and Health. He worked with his Swiss master (Le Corbusier) in which his work was inspired. His first major works were a series of buildings in Pampulha, suburb of Belo Horizonte. This work very well praised by national and foreign critics putting it in the spotlight. Throughout his career he has excelled with well organized and modern projects. His collaboration in the United Nations project earned him the invitation to teach at Yale University and Harvard University's design school.

In Brasilia, he designed the Brazilian National Congress, the Alvorada Palace, the Planalto Palace, the Supreme Federal Court and the Brasília Cathedral. This work led him to be appointed director of the architecture department of the University of Brasilia and Honorary member of the American Institute of Architects. Due to political dissent, he left the country after the military coup of 1964 opening an office in Paris. He returned to the country in 1985 and won the Pritzker Prize for Architecture in 1988. Some of his most recent projects were: The Museum of Contemporary Art of Niterói (1996), Oscar Niemeyer Museum in Curitiba (2002), the Administrative City of Minas Gerais) and the Oscar Niemeyer International Cultural Center (2011). He has always maintained an active life. He died on December 05, 2012 at the age of 104.

A COMPLETE ARTIST

Dolores Gonçalves Costa known artistically as Dercy Gonçalves was an actress, comedian and Brazilian singer having achieved recognition as the actress with the longest career in world history. Famous for her good humor and constant use of profanity was without a doubt the greatest exponent of the improvised theater in Brazil.

Of humble origin, was born in the interior of the state of Rio de Janeiro in 1905 and was registered only in 1907. This was common in Brazil at the time due to the difficulty of access to the notaries and lack of information about the importance of taking a document. Daughter of a tailor and a washerwoman, she was abandoned by her mother at the age of seven when she discovered her husband's infidelity. The little girl then had to face a chaotic family environment being raised by a drugged father. As a granddaughter of blacks, she suffered prejudice by being called a slave girl.

The girl soon had to work to help with the expenses of the house. Her first job was at a movie box office. This gave her the opportunity to get to know a bit of the artistic world and fall in love. She had a gift for art. The graduation in this area allows a contact with the different artistic branches such as music, dance and cinema preparing the student for the job market. This professional can work in cultural centers, galleries, museums, theaters, art schools, conservatories, companies of spectacle among others.

In order to fulfill his dream, she fled from her home to the city of Macaé when she was only seventeen years old under a train wagon risking her own life for her ideals. The reason for the escape was that she wanted to join a theater troupe who was there and could teach her the way to the art scene. She lived there for a while until the group moved to the state of Minas Gerais where they would make other presentations. She was together debuting in the year 1929 in the city of Leopoldina. The itinerant theater was her life and for that dreamy young woman everything was paying off.

Dercy first loved her work partner Eugenio Pascoal. The two were together when this lady of national royalty was twenty-five. The first sexual intercourse occurred some time later when she was convinced by the threat of termination.

Even after the loss of virginity, she remained with her innocent, joyful and childish spirit characteristics that ennobled this national born talent. Years later, because of jealousy, she separated from her boyfriend.

Her second romance was with coffee exporter Ademar Martins Senra. From this relationship was born her only daughter named Dercimar. Since she was married, they could not formally assume the relationship. It was then that she returned to work in the theater. In the professional field, she participated in the theater of Brazilian magazines in the thirties and forties. Already in the sixties, it debuted in the solo career. Her various performances in the theaters gradually gained a lively audience. Parallel to this work, she participated in films of the genre and national comedies. She has also participated in soap operas and TV programs.

The actress won in 1985 the Mambembe trophy in the category best theater character and was the theme of a samba school in 1991 at Unidos do Viradouro. Her biography was written by Maria Adelaide Amaral who also wrote a miniseries about her life. She passed away on July 19, 2008 at the age of one hundred and one.

A RENOWNED ARTIST

Candido Torquato Portinari was a well known Brazilian plastic artist. Throughout his career he painted approximately five thousand works with diversity, wealth and good taste. This area is recommended for those who have creativity, sensitivity and disposition to make use of visual and tactile elements such as drawings, paintings, engravings and sculptures. He handles various materials and technology. Generally your work is exposed in galleries, museums or in public. You can also work in the television area.

With an Italian family, he found it difficult at first to continue his studies or even to complete primary education. When he was fourteen, he had a great artistic opportunity: He was recruited as a helper by a group of Italian sculptors. It was the beginning of the professional trajectory of this great talent.

A year later, in search of his dream to develop his talent, he moved from São Paulo to Rio de Janeiro. He studied at the National School of Fine Arts. In a short time he was already prominent in the classroom and in the exhibitions he attended. He began to participate in contests and in 1928 he was awarded a medal and a trip to Europe.

He lived two years in Paris where he lived innovative experiences in the artistic and personal area. Returning to your country, it has completely changed. He begins to value colors better and leaves behind the three-dimensional drawing of his works. He starts in the area of murals and frescoes. After exhibiting in New York, his work was valued and he gained international notoriety.

Because of his frequent painting, the artist presented severe intoxication with lead, a material used in paints. It was recommended that he stop his activities, but contrary to medical orders he continued painting and traveling around the world. He ended up dying due to the worsening of this intoxication.

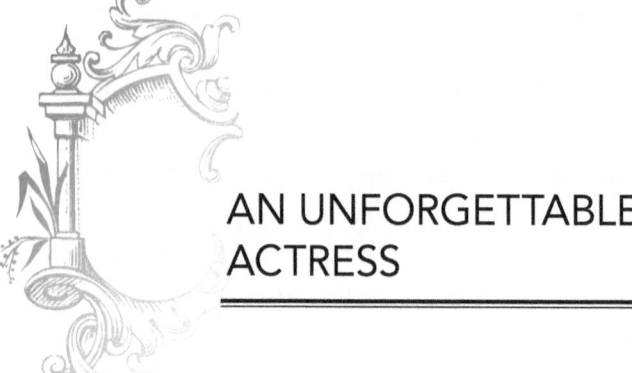

AN UNFORGETTABLE ACTRESS

Maria do Carmo Miranda da Cunha was an actress and Portuguese-Brazilian singer. Her professional career developed between the thirties and fifties in Brazil and the United States. She performed in radio, theater, film and television, showing a formidable performance. With her joy and irreverence he conquered the world. For those who want to pursue the career of an actress, the recommended course is the performing arts, which is the set of techniques used to create, assemble and interpret shows. Using the body movements and voice this professional develops characters capable of transmitting information and emotion to the public.

The success began in 1930 through a march song by Joubert de Carvalho. The success was so great that in a brief period she was already considered the most famous singer in the country. In the other year, she started an international tour in Argentina where she was also very successful. She returned to this country eight more times. During this same period, she signed a contract with a radio station and the success gave her the opportunity to participate in the first sound films.

When appearing in the cinema characterized of Baiana

gained international reputation. With this, she had the opportunity to participate in a show on Broadway. From its presentation, she began to be known as "The Brazilian Bombshell". In the 1940s, she made her American debut in the United States where she was very successful and came to be considered the third most popular personality in the country. In all, she participated in fourteen films in the United States between the forties and the fifties. Her presentations put Brazilian and Latin American culture in the spotlight abroad. She was our first artist to put her fingerprints at Grauman's Chinese Theater in 1941. She was also honored on the sidewalk of fame. The movement she pioneered is called tropicalism.

In a trajectory of twenty years of career left her recorded voice in three hundred and thirteen recordings. In her honor, a museum was erected in the capital of Rio.

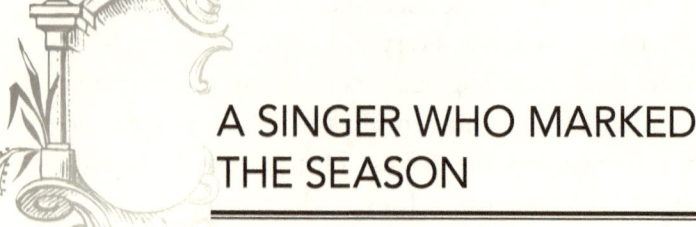

A SINGER WHO MARKED THE SEASON

Elis Regina was a Brazilian singer extremely recognized nationally and internationally. This area is recommended for those who have an aptitude for the arts and a beautiful vocal tone to delight people.

Her professional career began at the age of eleven on a radio program aimed at children's audiences called "The Guri Club". Turning out to be a great talent, the young lady already released her first LP at the age of sixteen.

In the sixties she was hired by Radio Gaúcha, traveled to Rio de Janeiro to record her first record, signed a contract with TV Rio to participate in programs, participated in the theater and as a TV presenter. Already in the seventies, she improved her musical gifts by recording discs with praiseworthy technical quality. She participated in the spectacle " False brilliant" that soon originated a disc reaching a great success. She participated in other shows also with a lot of repercussion.

She lived in a country of dictatorship where many musicians could not have the freedom of Expression that we have today being a fierce critique of this regime of government. Being very popular in society, this fact kept her away from prison.

Politically engaged, she participated actively in movements such as the campaign for the amnesty of Brazilian exiles and directly linked to the rights of Brazilian musicians. She died at age thirty-six on January 19, 1982 due to an overdose of cocaine and alcohol. Elis will always be in the heart of the Brazilians like a woman battling that always reached its ideals. She marked history.

CONSERVATION AND RESTORATION

André Torres, born in Piracicaba (interior of the state of são Paulo) in a low class family has always had the gift of care, delicacy and perception. Always interested in pursuing his studies despite the difficulties, he finished elementary school, high school and graduation in public schools, highlighting himself. The faculty chosen was the Baccalaureate in Conservation and Restoration. This area takes care of the preservation of buildings, objects and artistic works. This professional is able to recognize the historical and cultural value of books, photographs, paintings, sculptures, monuments, documents, landscapes, among others. He dominates the techniques of maintenance of these objects being able to act in organs of historical and artistic patrimony. An area that is always expanding.

Soon after graduating, he began to work in the labor market and achieved outstanding positions. With the money he got from work, he helped his family. Years later, he married and had children. He is an example of a dedicated, accomplished and happy young man. If you have the profile similar to his, invest in this area.

DANCE

Dance is an important form of expression for mastery over one's own body. This training allows the graduate to set up and direct shows and may also act as a dancer. In our country we have several examples of renowned professionals.

Franciele Ferreira was an example of this. Graduated in dance and performing arts was an actress and dancer. She has worked in the theater, television and cinema winning several important prizes. However, career success was not reflected in personal life. Married and mother of three, she had serious marital problems. Due to her partner's various betrayals, she contracted HIV and the complications of her illness led her to a premature death despite the consolidation of fame and success.

THE PRECURSOR OF BRAZILIAN DESIGN

Eliseu d'Angelo Visconti was a Brazilian painter, draftsman and designer. Of Italian origin, he came to Brazil in 1873 and lived in a farm. Receiving the affection of the hosts, he soon began to study in the capital Rio de Janeiro. He tried various crafts until he enrolled in the Imperial Academy of Fine Arts with renowned professors there. In 1890, he engaged in a revolution that would transform the institution into the National School of Fine Arts.

He stood out among the students earning a trip abroad. There he was admitted to the École normale d'enseignement du dessin (École Guérin), where he was pupil of Eugène Samuel Grasset considered a genius of the arts. At the same time, he attended the Julian Academy where he also had renowned masters. This consolidated formation reverberated in his works influenced by the movements symbolist, Impressionist and Art-nouveau. He travels to Madrid and exhibits in France returning to Brazil soon after. Here, he exposes his work in the then capital Rio de Janeiro. Already in 1903 he exhibits in São Paulo gaining national and international recognition.

He elaborated the works of decoration of the Municipal

Theater of Rio de Janeiro where at the time he won enough praise. He also took up a position at the National School of Fine Arts, but because of commitments abroad he asked for exemption. When returning definitively to Brazil, he created his own art reflected in the landscapes of Teresópolis. He passed away being considered an expert in his area formulating the fundamental basis for the creation of a profession that today is the designer in Brazil. This bachelor is responsible for creating and developing graphic projects involving objects and parts to be produced on a large scale.

PHOTOGRAPHY

Chico Albuquerque was a northeastern photographer. This area is intended for anyone who has ease of use of machines, films, lenses and the revelation techniques. You can work in newspapers, magazines, websites, television, movies and advertising agencies.

Son of photographers, he was interested in the area when making a short documentary. Later, he specialized and moved from Fortaleza to São Paulo where he opened his own studio. He was the pioneer in producing advertising campaigns in the country and bought the first equipment with Flash in 1958. Throughout his career, he participated in several exhibitions and national and international samples winning important prizes. He died a victim of an infarct leaving a vast work so that others who have affinity in this area mirror and continue to value the national culture.

A RESPECTED PHYSICIST

Albert Einstein was a German physicist. This area is suitable for those who have a passion for numbers and an investigative spirit. This professional studies the relations of the universe, its properties and laws, being able to act in industry or in general teaching. Born in Germany on March 14, 1879, he was the son of Jews. His father and uncle founded an electrical equipment company and a year later his parents had his younger sister. At the age of five, the young boy has been enrolled in a Catholic school. Three years later, he was transferred to a gymnasium currently baptized with his name in his honor. There, he studied primary and secondary. Seven years later, he left Germany. His curiosity began to be aroused through his uncle who was an engineer and a friend who was a medical student.

With the bankruptcy of his father's firm, his family had to move to Italy where they settled in Milan and a while later in Pavia. Meanwhile, he was studying in Munich. Using a medical certificate, he was released from school activities by going to his parents' house. At this time he wrote a short essay. At the age of sixteen, he took an admission exam for the Swiss Federal Polytechnic School, achieving high marks in physics and mathematics. It was his first great achievement even though at the time he did not complete his regular schooling afterwards at the Cantonal School.

He enrolled in a course in order to obtain a Physics teacher's degree. Mileva Maric was the only woman of the course and together they developed a friendship and later a romance. In 1900, he will get the diploma. The two were married on January 6, 1903, in Bern. A year later, the first child was born. Already the second son was born in 1910 in Zurich. Although he was married, evidence shows that he was not happy nurturing the desire for an old love.

He returned to Germany in 1914 in the city of Berlin. His wife and children stayed in Switzerland. The inevitable divorce occurred on February 14, 1919. The main reason was the constant fights of the couple provoked by jealousy. He remarried on June 2, 2019 with Elsa Löwenthal. In the year 1933, they moved to the United States where two years later she passed away. Of his sons with his first wife, he had only one grandchild. He continued his career in this country until the last days of his life.

A GENIUS NAMED NEWTON

Isaac Newton was an astronomer, physicist, mathematician, alchemist, philosopher and theologian. His work was recognized as one of the most influential in the history of science. In this area he revolutionized knowledge until then in describing the law of gravitation and three laws. If you have a creative and investigative profile the astronomy area is perfect for you. This science studies the universe and its animate or inanimate components. The astronomer develops theories by testing them in practice. The field of this professional can take place in the observation of the cosmos or in the attempt to explain the origin of the universe.

Newton's contribution to humanity is immense. He built the first telescope, developed the theory of colors, elaborated the empirical law of cooling, studied the speed of sound, worked with infinitesimal calculus, contributed to the study of power series, developed Newton's method for approximation of the roots of a function, generalized the binomial theorem among others. He also studied alchemy and biblical chronology. Anyway, it marked history.

IN THE COMPUTER AGE

Bill Wiliam was born in the computer age. American middle-class, always had at disposal the technological devices and fell in love with it. Living in a city like New York, he does not stop going out with friends, going out with his girlfriend, working and traveling. At one point, he was fired and then made a serious decision. He decided to specialize and the chosen graduation was the science of computing. Whoever he is trained in this works in the elaboration of computer programs. By developing programs and applications, he manages other creators and systems. He can operate in all sectors of the economy.

What was once just a diversion became a source of income for him. From there, with the knowledge gained, you can grow professionally and this is reflected in his personal life. He married, helped his parents, had children and began to dedicate himself to them. He learned to value the good things in life better, not losing his essence as a good boy. Do as he does and decide which way to go.

A REMARKABLE NATURALIST

Charles Robert Darwin was a British naturalist scientist who through his theories revolutionized the concepts of scientific society of the time. Taking an analogy with the present epoch, a faculty proposed for this profile is the bachelor's degree in science and technology. This professional should have a solid background in exact sciences and engineering principles. The labor market is broad: Financial area, industry, technology companies, public agencies, third sector, etc. Currently, the government strongly encourages research through scholarships.

Born in Shrewsbury on February 12, 1809, he was the fifth of his sons. With a wealthy background, his family belonged to the elite of the time. Upon losing his mother early, he was sent to the local school. His interest was concentrated in the small animals of the most varied specimens showing a spectacular gift of observation. In 1825, he studied medicine at the University of Edinburgh. From the second year of graduation, he began to participate in naturalistic groups revealing a growing desire for the area. Working together with Robert Edmond Grant has developed interesting theories about marine animals. He also studied stratigraphic geology and the classification of plants developing recognized and very interesting works.

This great man despite his engagement with the sciences

frustrated the parents' desire to see him trained as a doctor. He was then enrolled in the Cambridge University Arts course. However, instead of studying, he focused on the observation of the field, especially the small beetles. It was then that he enrolled in the Natural History course performing above-expected.

Trying to evade rapid ordering, he attended Geology being named assistant in stratigraphic mapping in Wales. His first plans of trip to the island of the wood did not work being him relocated to another adventure destined to South America. This expedition lasted five years, which had a profound impact on science.

In this unique opportunity, this naturalist studied geological characteristics, organisms and people. He managed to collect several specimens hitherto unknown to Europeans. His extensive research has strengthened his professional career. In his treatise "The Journey of Begle" he documented all his observations, impressions, and findings. In later editions, the theory of evolution was proposed. Although highly contradictory to a time dominated by the religious axis, his ideas provoked much discussion and involved all sectors of society.

Darwin was acclaimed by the scientific community for his theory and studies. Of course, he married and had ten children. Many of them also achieved great prestige. This genius passed away on April 19, 1882.

MATHEMATICAL AND LAND SCIENCES

Pierre de Fermat was a French scientist and mathematician. One proposed college for anyone who has a penchant for this area is the undergraduate degree in mathematics and earth science. Who completes this course is qualified in mathematics, physics and science. Its field is broadly able to operate in the financial market or in any market that involves mathematical analysis.

Son of a fur merchant, good financial condition provided him access to education. He finished his studies and soon began to work in the public service. Little by little, he grew up on the professional scale and made his way to the Judge's post. Due to the limitations of the time and the habitual shyness of this gentleman his discoveries were only published well afterwards. His superior intellect put to the test by several times did not fail by putting it in prominence and recognition.

Among his great achievements are the invention of analytic geometry, the development of geometric and infinitesimal calculus, he contributed in number theory and probability theory. Despite his great recognition as a mathematician this was never his main activity. His official profession was a magistrate, as already quoted. The math was reserved for their hours off. Even so, he was the greatest mathematician of his day. He died on cots, city of France.

A RENOWNED STATISTICIAN

Karl Pearson was an important name that made a great contribution to world statistics. Who graduates in this degree has a wide area focused on the collection, analysis and interpretation of data related to natural, economic and social phenomena. Acting in the planning, coordination and information gathering this professional uses several techniques such as the questionnaire, interviews and measurements. With the data in hand he interprets and organizes a database for current and future use. His work has great application in the industry in general.

His most relevant works were in the areas of biology, epidemiology, anthropometry, medicine and social history. His studies have built on the classical statistical methods currently used. Among his contributions we can cite: In linear regression and correlation, in the classification of distributions, chi-square test, and correlation coefficient and asymmetry coefficients. He really marked our history.

THE MODERN MEDICINE

Patrick Adams is a renowned doctor on the west coast of England. Come from middle class family, he always believed that his mission would be to revolutionize and protect human life. He is an adept of nanotechnology in therapeutic processes. But what would that be? This is a science that develops technological processes from tiny particles in the dimension scale of atoms. The areas involved in this work are research, from medicine to computing. Specifically in medicine, our noble colleague believes in improving vision, combating degenerative brain diseases, improving cardiac output, altering genes in order to avoid congenital diseases and the probable immortality achieved through the action of nanorobots.

He is a worldwide leader in his field and believes that his commitment can transform the world in a meaningful way. Do as he does and strive with your profile to do a good job and achieve recognition. Good luck is what I wish for everyone.

THE FATHER OF MODERN CHEMISTRY

Antonie Laurent de Lavoisier was a man of the past specialized in Chemistry considered the progenitor of this science. It is up to the chemist to study matter, its composition and its properties. Analyzing the physicochemical compounds such as hardness or toxicity, this professional evaluates the characteristics of the chemical reactions. His field of work is in the industry. The student profile for this type of course is investigative, insightful and creative.

Born into a noble family, he always had the best opportunities that life has provided. From a young age, he studied chemistry, botany, astronomy and mathematics. Coupled with a great dedication on his part, the result was quite satisfactory. Following the precepts of the time, he married one of his class, an aristocrat named Marie Anne Pierrete Paulze. With her help, his scientific works could be translated. He enunciated the principle of conservation of matter and baptized oxygen. In addition, he participated in the chemical nomenclature. He was guillotined on May 8, 1794, ending a successful trajectory.

A FANTASTIC ARCHAEOLOGIST

Howard Carter was one of the most prominent archaeologists in history. This professional is responsible for studying the human cultures of the past. The labor market is concentrated in research centers, universities or in major works.

His first professional experience happened when he was seventeen when he was an assistant in excavations and archaeological records. He did very well in the area by highlighting himself in this and other works. His great feat that went down in history was to have found the tomb of Pharaoh Tutankhamun and his riches. He died peacefully for having marked the story.

THE VALUE OF COOPERATION

The hope community in the rural area of Pesqueira-Brasil is a group of recent settlers of agrarian reform. United through an association, they always combine actions for the benefit of all. This is called cooperativism. The student who graduates in this area after the course must master techniques in the creation, implantation, analysis, administration and focus on general results focusing on the common good. He has to know a little about public policies, economics and education by applying the data to lead the cooperative. Unity is strength and this should be taken as a lesson for all segments. Do as the group hope.

A GREAT JURIST

Ruy Barbosa de Oliveira was a jurist, politician, diplomat, writer, translator and speaker. For those who long to excel as he should attend law school. This is the science that takes care of the correct application of legal norms prevailing in a country. The goal is to maintain harmony between individuals in a society.

Born in Salvador-Bahia-Brazil, he was the nephew of the Baron de Mucuri and the governor of the state. By the time he was five, he had excelled at school impressing his masters with his talent. When he was eleven, he stood out even more winning a medal of honor to merit. As an adult, he joined the law school of Olinda. He finished his degree at the Law School of Largo de São Francisco. He returned to his already diseased province. Then he got better and started to advocate. A year later, he began a journalistic career. Years later, he married and was elected deputy by the assembly of his state. He was important in promoting a comprehensive education reform.

When he was appointed Finance Minister, he tried to erase the stain of slavery by having the records of the slaves burned. However, this was only a strategy for not paying compensation to landlords with the end of slavery in the country. He was also responsible for the crenelling crisis. He was appointed shortly afterwards as first deputy head of government and ended up leaving the post by disappointing himself with the regime of the government. He returned to Bahia. A revolt broke out and forced him to take refuge in Chile. Still fearful, he moved to Buenos Aires.

In 1894, he is candidate to the president obtaining the fourth place. He then travels to London from where he sends correspondence to a Brazilian newspaper exercising his journalistic vein. Becomes a founding member of the Brazilian Academy of Letters. In 1907, he consecrated himself worldwide when participating in the Conference of The Hague. He influenced the disputed war by supporting the state of Paraná.

At other times, he applied for the presidency of the republic. However, he was defeated. He demands a stance of the neutral countries during the First World War becoming famous and in 1917 participates in the project "Brazilian Translation". Already in 1918 he gains the French insignia of great officer of the National order of the Legion of Honor. He passed away in 1923 having marked a glorious history. Actually he was a great man.

A JOKE TO OTHERS

Henrique Mateus has always been the family joke. Born from a middle-class family, the son of a lawyer and a doctor, he was the only one in the family not to have a profession or to be so valued. He is a graduate in home economics. The activities developed by him aim to improve people's quality of life. He plans, develops and implements programs in the areas of food, consumer rights, family economics, housing, health and clothing. He can act as manager in restaurants or organize spaces for members of a company.

The choice of their profession generated the revolt of the parents and they fought ugly. He, however, did not care. He was happy with himself and despite not having a life so quiet financially speaking he had a peaceful mind. With the money from his labor, he got married and can support his family. What matters is that it was a decent job and he wanted to show his family someday. Until that day came, he would go on.

A BLACK SYMBOL

Martin Luther King Jr. was a political activist and a Protestant pastor. A college recommended for those who have a profile similar to his is the one of studies of gender and diversity. The work of this professional is to act in public policies focusing on human and social diversity. He generally seeks to engage in still problematic issues such as equal rights for men and women, ethnic diversity, various sexual orientations and age groups. He can work in public agencies, cooperatives, NGOs or companies.

Born in Georgia, he soon began his campaign against discrimination against blacks in his day. He was arrested and threatened with death, but he did not give up so easily because his ideals were greater than fear. Acting as a pastoral leader, he emphasized his cause by organizing peaceful demonstrations against the laws of society in force. Their efforts were rewarded with a greater debate on civil rights.

He fought like a great hero by the right to vote, the end of the racial segregation, the end of the discriminations, against the poverty and other rights. In the future, their claims were consolidated with the approval of the Civil Rights Act (1964) and the Electoral Rights Act (1965). For his great achievements, he was awarded the Nobel Peace Prize in 1964. However, on April 4, 1968, he was cowardly murdered. He died but entered into history as a symbol of black resistance.

AN ETHNO DEVELOPMENT ACTIVIST

Dorothy Mae Stang was an American nunnery based in Brazil who was fighting for ethno-development in the Amazon region. Those who work in this area struggle for the development and preservation of cultural diversity. Understanding of ethnic relations, she seeks to improve the lives of populations through sustainable projects. In order to do this, she analyzes the social context, taking care of the protection of natural resources, mediating the contact between the population and the public agencies.

In 1950, she entered the religious life and issued definitive vows in 1956. She worked for fifteen years as a teacher at the congregation school and at the end of this period she moved to Brazil. Here, she came to perform a beautiful mission. Through pastoral activity, she aimed at sustainable development and the reduction of land conflicts. For her determination and courage she gained national and international fame. A great achievement was the founding of the first teacher education school in the Amazon region, which brought about a greater development. Despite constant death threats, she was not intimidated and continued her work. She was murdered on February 12, 2005 leaving a memorable legacy. Undoubtedly, one of the most important women in our history.

SOCRATES

Socrates was a renowned philosopher who lived in Greece as the founder of Western philosophy. The faculty of philosophy is intended for curious instigators who ask themselves the question of life. Its function is to question the essence of the universe through a critical analysis. Studying the thought and works of philosophers, the student seeks the theoretical understanding of general concepts. He can work in scientific, artistic and cultural institutions.

Coming of humble origin, he was the son of a sculptor and a midwife. However, his fate was different by discovering his vocation as an educator with his mother's help. He married and had three children. Some of his characteristics were: He walked barefoot, he did not take a shower, he liked to meditate and read.

Learning from great masters he was considered the wisest man in his country. What he advocated was always a permanent investigation with priority over the transfer of knowledge. He used to lecture in public places giving attention to all his disciples which denoted his popular character. Unfortunately, for political reasons, he was condemned and executed. However, he wrote an important chapter in the history of mankind.

A FAMOUS GEOGRAPHER

Erthostenes of Cyrene was a great man of ancient Greece who stood out as a geographer, mathematician and astronomer. Who graduates in Geography is able to study the earth and its occupation by man. The area covers physical geography and the way people relate to the environment. As a teacher, he works in primary, secondary and higher education.

In the professional field, he wrote several philosophical works, poems, mathematical stories and grammatical works. His contribution is relevant in mathematics and the humanities. His greatest was to have calculated accurately the measure of the circumference of the earth. He is also considered the founder of the geography discipline. He passed away being one of the most important men in the world.

HISTORIAN

Marc Leopold Benjamin Bloch is considered the greatest historian of all time. Those who form this study the human past in its different aspects. His work consists basically of field research. Being licensed, you can teach.

Son of a teacher, he was very diligent in his studies. He graduated in the best schools of Paris. He participated of the First World War and after he founded a magazine that brought him worldwide success. With the outbreak of World War II he had to leave the direction of the magazine. Acting in the resistance he was arrested and shot on June 16, 1944. His greatest historical contribution was in the area of feudalism.

A LITTLE BIT OF THE LITTLE DREAMER OF THE CAVE

Aldivan Teixeira Torres also known as Divinha, son of God, seer or little dreamer is a Brazilian writer. A recommended graduation for anyone who wants to follow in this area is graduation in letters. The course is for those who wish to dedicate themselves to the study of Mother tongue and foreign languages. Upon graduation, he has his license to teach in schools. Another field of work is in the editors in services of revision, preparation of originals and translation.

I am myself. I do not have much importance in literature yet, but I consider myself a hero in the face of all that I have lived and I want to share some of my experience with you. Well, let's go. Born into a poor family in the hinterland region of northeastern Brazil, I lived from poverty, neglect, indifference and lack of hope. I have five brothers older than me. We are a family of farmers and just before I was born my brothers had to leave school to help support the family. They went to the state of Paraíba to work on tomato plantations. In the midst of sun, rain, poison, they had to work hard to give us a better life. At that time, education was not held with great importance and this was a common reality in our midst. It was with this money that my father was able to buy the place we live in today.

I did not have an easy life either. Even though I had the opportunity to study, I was going to help the farm and, because I was fragile, I would often come back with a fever and tired. Seeing my fragility, my father freed me from work and then I concentrated only on studies. However, I did not have the least financial support from them. What I had was just a strong will to win. The difficulty of didactic material was circumvented by the opening of a community library in my village. I could then study better and have access to history books. I loved and I love books. I read them quickly and ended entire collections. This improved my writing style by highlighting me at school with maximum grade essays. One day a teacher wrote to me: This will still be a great man.

I was still far from my goal simply because my financial conditions were lousy. My first experience in literature was when I collected some excerpts from the books of Ecclesiastes, wisdom, folk tales, and I made the book. I showed my colleagues very proudly as if it were mine. But I had no incentive. The answer they gave me was that the texts were not mine and therefore had no merit at all. It was the first dismay of my literary career. Even so, I would not give up so easily from my dream. I went ahead with my life.

I finished high school, I took a computer course, I went to a technical course in electricity where I learned about this area in two years. The moment I was about to train, I was stopped by a mysterious force. The period of three years later was the worst moment of my life. An instant in which I delved into the dark night of the soul that inspired me to write a novel later.

In the dark night, I forgot my good principles and I only committed sins. Leisure was my biggest challenge and I had no prospect of improvement. I got to the point that I had no more hopes with the coming darkness to win my soul. Before

I surrendered myself a wonderful force manifested itself and delivered me from all evil. From there I was assured of the love of the father being named by the forces of the good of "Son of God." I promised a sincere change and I entered into communion with the forces of light. Things have gradually improved.

I went to college, got a job, and wrote my first book giving an answer to those who did not believe in my gift. It was not yet the time of full literature but it was a divine sign that I should not be completely discouraged. The four years of undergraduate mathematics have developed my cognitive and perceptive reasoning. During school vacations I wrote my first novel, taking the village I live in to this day. But I still could not fully devote myself to my dream because of professional and school commitments.

Upon completion of college, I passed on a better contest and then resumed the hope of writing freely. I started working seriously on my project. Today, I have more than ten completed works and walking for more. My purpose is to write as long as possible. My goal is to enchant the hearts and encourage reading around the world. My cause is just and I hope that my spiritual father will continue to bless me as he has done so far. I am a winner.

A LEADING MUSEOLOGIST

Clovis Bornay was a celebrated museologist and carnival. The professional trained in museology is dedicated to the cataloging, conservation, selection and exhibition of important pieces. Its purpose is to spread knowledge and preserve it for future generations. He also acts in the public policies directed to the historical-cultural patrimony of humanity. His field of work is in museums, universities, community centers or archaeological sites.

Son of a Spanish mother and Swiss father, he was the youngest of his children out of a total of twelve. It was in his youth that his passion for carnival emerged as a pioneer in the institution of carnival dances with costumes competitions. In the first edition, he came in first. He also began to parade in schools of samba becoming a master in costumes of carnauba cariocas. He has won numerous fancy contests and carnivals. As a singer, he recorded marches for the carnival in the sixties and seventies. He had also participated in the movies.

As a museologist, he worked for forty-two years at the National Historical Museum. However, his great passion was the arts. A man worthy of being remembered forever.

THE PATRON OF BRAZILIAN EDUCATION

Paulo Reglus Neves Freire was a Brazilian philosopher, educator and pedagogue. The graduation in pedagogy refers to the knowledge of the principles and methods of teaching, of the performance in schools and in relation to the educational subjects in general. The goal is always to improve teaching. The trainee can act in the teaching profession or administration.

Born in Recife, son of a military police captain, he had a sister and two brothers. One worked as a teacher, one in the city hall of Recife and the other in the army. Due to the fact that his siblings had worked at an early age, this allowed him to continue his studies.

Despite being born into a middle-class family, the young man experienced misery in the depression of 1929. The experience led him to worry about the poor and to devise a new method of literacy. His dedication to the humblest has made him an example all over the world.

Graduated in law, he never exercised the profession preferring to act as a Portuguese Language teacher. On several occasions, he had the practical opportunity to build a method of literacy that had encouraging results. As a result, this project has been expanded with government support. However, with the outbreak of the military coup, his work was canceled. He was exiled spending time in Bolivia and Chile. It was at this time that he published his first book entitled "Education as a practice of freedom". The work was a critical success bringing him an even greater prominence by being invited to be visiting professor at Harvard University.

The amnesty in 1979 made it possible for him to return to Brazil. He has worked in several commissioned positions related to education where he did a beautiful job. With the death of his wife, he remarried and founded an institute to propagate his ideas. He passed away on May 2, 1997 due to complications in surgery. He was one of the most recognized Brazilians in history earning twenty-nine Doctor Honoris causa titles among other awards.

PSYCHOPEDAGOGY

Jorge Pedro Luís Visca was an Argentine psycho-pedagogue. This professional studies the learning processes identifying the obstacles that interfere in the assimilation of the contents. In cases of school failure, he promotes interventions in order to improve teaching. Your field of work can be in hospitals, community centers or offices.

He was the main promoter of his profession in his country and abroad. In his professional line he followed three lines: School of Geneva, Psychoanalytic School and Social Psychology. He founded and accompanied psychopedagogical centers in Brazil and Argentina. He is also the author of several books with themes related to his area. For his great contribution, he received several honors and awards. He was a really important man.

INTERNATIONAL RELATIONS

Humberto can be defined as a young man with a negotiating, critical, managerial and human profile. These qualities have made him choose to graduate in international relations. Who is formed in this leads the relationship between peoples, nations and organizations in several areas. By analyzing the world scenario, you are able to choose the best investment path. It also promotes understandings between entities from different countries. He can work in ministries, embassies and ONGs.

With a great choice of profession, Beto can establish firm roots in the professional and personal fields. At leisure times, he enjoys life with family and friends as it should be. He is a cheerful, optimistic and persuasive boy who helps to succeed in all endeavors. Do as he does and choose the right path.

SOCIAL WORKER

Karen is a Brazilian who works as a social worker at the National Institute of Social Security. The generic assignments of a social worker are to plan and execute public policies and social programs aimed at integrating the individual into society. Its objective is to improve the life of the most needy sections of the population through project proposals. Her work is fundamental in the area of government assistance.

Karen is more than a professional in her work living harmoniously with her colleagues. She is also confident and merciful to her clients. For her good deeds, she was recognized with the award of best attendant of her company. This also reflected in the personal field with her living a great union with the husband and children. If you have a profile similar to hers, a degree in social work is the best way to go.

AN ANCIENT THEOLOGIAN

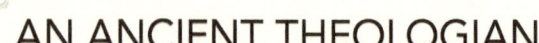

Augustine of Hippo was an important philosopher and theologian of early Christianity. The theologian studies religions and their influence on society. Researching historical facts related to religion is capable of interpreting and applying them in the current context. He works as a researcher or advisor in religious groups. Having a degree, he can teach in schools, ONGs and centers linked to religiosity.

Born in Roman Africa, his mother was a Christian and his father a pagan. Early on, when I was eleven, I began to study Latin literature and pagan beliefs and practices. He also aroused interest in philosophy. Already at seventeen, he moved to Carthage where he was able to study rhetoric. Although raised in the Christian precepts, he was interested in knowing other aspects enriching in knowledge. He is also remembered as a young man for his hedonistic stance in a world still repressive in sexual matters.

He maintained for thirteen years a relationship in concubinage that had as fruit a son considered as intelligent as the father. In his professional life, he was Grammar teacher and director of a school of rhetoric from which he left to found his own school. Disappointed with the behavior of students who do not even paid classes. That is where he went to serve at the imperial court standing out in the Latin academic world.

Sometime later, he became definitive to Christianity. His companion and his son died which caused him considerable pain. He decided to sell everything and to donate to the poor keeping only the family house living a monastic life. The religious interest increased, he was ordained priest and with little time of work he became very famous. Later, he was ordained bishop and took over the episcopal throne that only left with the death. Characterized as a dedicated person, who ate little, hated gossip, he avoided the things of the world and prudently he was really a remarkable man of his day. He passed away having marked the history of Christianity definitively.

A RECOGNIZED BAIANO TRANSLATOR

Rogério Duarte Guimarães was a translator, teacher, composer, graphic artist, musician and writer. The interpreter and translator transcribe texts and speeches from one language to another. The interpreter translates orally and the translator translates graphically. Graduation in this area prepares students to face challenges and master the colloquial and formal language of their target languages. Being able to specialize in the various required areas.

From Bahia he moved to Rio de Janeiro in the sixties where he began studying industrial art. He worked as a director of publishing house and graphic artist for film promotion. He was also one of the mentors of the Tropicalist movement being tortured and imprisoned during the military regime.

He studied Eastern customs having translated the Sanskrit Bhagavad Gita. In addition, he launched the book tropicaos, a biographical book, where he tells a little about the movement he created and his personal experience of the military regime. He died of cancer at seventy-seven years of age.

ARCHIVIST

Alzira Vargas do Amaral Peixoto was a Brazilian archivist. This is the professional responsible for organizing, evaluating and restoring documents to be recorded on paper or image in any media or database. She can work in companies, government agencies, schools, associations, ONGs or health institutions.

Daughter of former president Getúlio Vargas, she was her father's private archivist since 1932. Seven years later, she married a federal auditor with whom she had a daughter. She acted along with him as messenger of her father next to the government of the United States.

With the beginning of redemocratization, she played an important role in politics and advised her father until the end of his days. Her husband was governor of Rio de Janeiro and after his departure appointed ambassador to the United States. Alzira went with him there. Upon returning to Brazil, she wrote her father's biography. She died on January 26, 1992.

LIBRARIAN

Jorge Francisco Isidoro Luis Borges was a librarian, translator, poet, literary critic, teacher, writer and essayist. Argentine. The undergraduate degree in Librarianship prepares students to classify, select, organize and care for libraries. He manages the entire collection by implementing improvements and managing data. The field of work is broad, in addition to libraries can work in museums, publishing houses, research centers among others. The student profile is administrator type, perfectionist, curious and zealous.

Born into a wealthy and traditional family, he soon came into contact with the world of letters through a good family and societal education. He fell in love with the books and promised himself that he would be a writer. He moved to Europe with this desire. He was in Switzerland and Spain. Afterwards, he returned to his homeland. He then began his professional career by publishing his first book. From then on it he did not stop. He also worked as director of the National Library.

Approaching a chaotic theme set in what would be today "Fantastic Literature", his books were short texts linked by the same theme. With translation of his works in the United States and in Europe he gained international recognition. As a publisher, he also excelled in winning several important awards. He passed away leaving the story set forever.

CINEMA AND AUDIOVISUAL

Alfred Joseph Hitchcock was a great icon of world cinema. His role was filmmaker. Who carries out this work directs and creates products for the cinema, TV or Internet. Being able to act in all stages of production, this area is destined for those who love the arts, entertainment and fun.

Born in London, he was the son of a merchant. Despite his father's humility, this was a striking figure throughout his life inspiring him to fight for his ideals and helping him in what would be later in the film set. His childhood can be characterized as a happy childhood despite authoritarianism and often transgression present in the head of his family.

Shortly thereafter, they moved to Poplar and Stepney. On both occasions, the boy sedimented his school education by coming into contact with the world itself in its political, cultural, historical and religious contexts.

His world was a backward, rigid, and extreme intolerant world. In the historical accounts the role of an education that was punitive to the extreme is very clear. Unlike today's concept, it is about interconnection, intercommunication, enhancement and respect most of the time.

At the age of fourteen, he left elementary school and excelled in the performance of the most important subjects. He was a cheerful, entwined and playful boy making him win over everyone in this period. He took this his way for the rest of his life by inspiring him in the movies.

After leaving basic school, he concentrated on the professional field when he started his degree in Engineering and a drawing course. It was from there that came the interest in the cinema until then an entertainment in their hours off. With the death of the father, new responsibilities came and a formal job was the option to support the family. From the twenties on, he actually started in the artistic area. He began as a lyricist and then with the emergence of an opportunity became director. Thus began a meteoric career recognized throughout the world. Through his genius, he has contributed many innovations to this medium. He passed away having left a consolidated mark.

THE EDU-COMMUNICATOR

André Viçosa was born in a poor community of Luziânia-Goiás-Brazil. As soon as people were understood, he faced immense difficulties in relation to school education. He had to attend public school and face the precariousness of a school system that does not yet adequately shape the world of work.

The obstacles were a challenge for him and the will to win increased more and more. He completed high school, college and other study placements being the pride of the family. He decided to act in edu-communication which for him would be a way of helping others. Those without form in the area use the various means of communication to design and implement projects related to the area of education. Its specific activities can be carried out in ONGs, communication vehicles, educational institutions and public agencies. Being licensed, you can also be a high school teacher.

The glorious André stood out in the area being respected in the educational environment throughout the world. He also uses his experience to give lectures and train other educators. He established his family base and taught his children the basic values of a good man highlighting the claw, hope, persistence and faith in their own potentialities. He is considered a great man.

BACHELOR OF MEDIA STUDIES

Ellen Rochele is a young woman from Salvador, from a traditional family, who grew up full of doubts about which profession to follow. She took a vocational test and could not even set her course. An unusual fact happened while watching a movie together with her boyfriend. It was an action movie and romance and a melancholy ending of the main characters disappointed her and gave her possibilities for change. That was when a crack came and she decided that she would try her degree in media studies.

The following year, she had a college degree and was awarded a degree in one of the first places. The period of study only reaffirmed the suspicions of vocation and she remained studying until completing it. At the end, she married and began her professional career. This course enables the person to have knowledge about the media and the way they act in society. The field of work is vast: Radio, TV, Written press and internet. She can work in different positions within a company. The appropriate profile for those who want to take this degree is creativity, curiosity, teamwork and research.

With personal and professional happiness, the young woman continued her life gaining recognition and important prizes. Who would have thought that chance would lead her on the right path? This life is really amazing.

INFORMATION MANAGEMENT

André Leone was born in a wealthy family from São Paulo. Within a family environment of rare tranquility and in traditional schools he developed a healthy and peculiar temperament. With skills in analysis, observation and organization he decided to pursue a degree in information management. The professional trained in this is responsible for collecting, processing and distributing information. He analyzes the market using statistical data to verify the viability of a business.

Already graduated, he has developed a beautiful professional career and allied with it a consistent love life. Happy in these two fields, he can then live and be fulfilled. As soon as he had children, he taught them the steps to be a good citizen. He was truly to be congratulated.

A RENOWNED JOURNALIST

Francisco de Assis Chateaubriand Bandeira de Mello was a journalist, entrepreneur, writer and politician among other professions. The job of a journalist is to seek information with the intention of disseminating them in the media. He can work on writing a written or spoken newspaper. The profile for this professional requires dedication, investigation, curiosity and critical sense.

Born into a stabilized family, his name is a tribute to the saint of the day he was born. Already the surname has originated in the admiration that the family had by the French thinker René de Chateaubriand. He married once and had only three children.

In his professional career, he graduated in law with a degree in journalism at the age of fifteen. He wrote for two newspapers in Recife. Moving to Rio de Janeiro, he collaborated for "The Morning Mail". A little later, he took over the direction of another newspaper and bought it later. Gradually, he bought important newspapers from different capitals, forming a real journalistic empire. By the end of his career he had thirty-four newspapers, thirty-six radio stations, eighteen TV stations, a news agency, weekly and monthly magazines and a publishing house. He was famous for journalistic devices in order to gain notoriety and prestige and by using the most advanced technologies in his companies.

He was truly a great journalistic and cultural personality. Due to a thrombosis, he became paraplegic. Even so, he remained active until his death. He died but entered into history.

MULTIMEDIA

Ellen Pereira was born at the time of technological explosions. From an early age she learned to deal with these modern revolutions and did very well in practice and theory. Her passion was so great that he graduated in multimedia. Work in this area is related to digital media. Defining, organizing and planning strategies, the professional executes projects used on the internet. She usually works in an integrated team with other professionals in the area.

Having a good role in the work, the young woman gained recognition and was also consolidated in the personal life. All of this has shown that full success is possible as long as one strives. The important thing is to choose well so that you do not regret it later.

CULTURAL PRODUCER
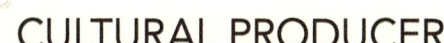

Pedro Gonzalez was a Mexican in love with the arts. He chose for himself as a profession to be a cultural producer. His attributions are to organize spectacles be it of theater, dance, music, television, festivals and cultural events. In addition, he can act in the area of cultural investments.

For being hardworking and inventive, he has consolidated himself as a great organizer of events gaining national and international prestige. As a result he has won several important awards. Already in personal life by his way playful and free of being never got a serious relationship. This is not to say that he never loved. He had many good experiences. At the end of his life, he rested happily from all his labors getting eternal through his works.

EDITORIAL PRODUCER

André Rebelo joined the publishing industry as a second option. His dream was to be a writer, but because he did not have much creativity or language skills, he chose to work for a publisher. He works in the editing and publishing stages of works of the most varied genres. He also has the role of defining the published titles, content, format and cover of the work. In short, he is an engineer in book production.

Failure as an author has provided him with a great performance as a producer, which has earned him several honors in this medium. Here is the example that not always what we think is the most appropriate for our career.

ADVERTISING

Leticia Meireles has always shown herself to be an artifice in sales. Her ease of communication and persuasion led her to choose the advertising faculty. Upon completion of the course, she was prepared to work in the area. The job is to present campaigns and advertising pieces aimed at marketing some product. In addition, it researches the consumer profile by designing strategies to achieve their preference. If you do not achieve the goals, you remake the strategy always aiming for the greatest possible profit.

It was also in the work that she conquered a husband using her techniques and the best, knew how to keep her by her side. We all have to have some of her skills to achieve success like hers.

www.ingramcontent.com/pod-product-compliance
Lightning Source LLC
Chambersburg PA
CBHW020543080526
44583CB00013B/975